BULLETPOINTS

OCEANS & RIVERS

John Farndon
Consultant: Peter Riley

BYEWAY
B O O K S

First published in 2004 by Miles Kelly Publishing Ltd
Bardfield Centre, Great Bardfield
Essex, CM7 4SL

This 2005 edition published by Byeway Books
Byeway Books Inc.
Lenexa, KS 66219, 866-4BYEWAY
www.byewaybooks.com

Editorial Director: Belinda Gallagher

Editor: Isla MacCuish

Design: WhiteLight

Picture Research: Liberty Newton

Production: Estela Boulton, Elizabeth Brunwin

Library of Congress Cataloging-in-Publication Data
is on file at the Library of Congress.

ISBN 1-933581-01-8

Printed in China

2 4 6 8 10 9 7 5 3 1

The publishers would like to thank the following artists who have contributed to this book:
Gary Hincks, Janos Marffy, Guy Smith

The publishers would also like to thank the following source for the use of their photograph:
Page 38 Ralph White/CORBIS

Contents

Rivers

- **Rivers** are filled with water from rainfall running directly off the land, from melting snow or ice, or from a spring bubbling out water that is soaked into the ground.

- **High up in mountains** near their source (start), rivers are usually small. They tumble over rocks through narrow valleys which they carved out over thousands of years.

▲ *A river typically tumbles over boulders high up near its source.*

- **All the rivers** in a certain area, called a catchment area, flow down to join each other, like branches on a tree. The branches are called tributaries. The bigger the river, the more tributaries it is likely to have.

- **As rivers flow downhill,** they are joined by tributaries and grow bigger. They often flow in smooth channels made not of big rocks but of fine debris washed down from higher up. River valleys are wider and gentler lower down, and the river may wind across the valley floor.

- **In its lower reaches** a river is often wide and deep. It winds back and forth in meanders (see river channels) across broad floodplains made of silt from higher up.

- **Rivers flow fast** over rapids in their upper reaches. On average, they flow as fast in the lower reaches where the channel is smoother because there is much less turbulence.

- **Rivers wear away** their banks and beds, mainly by battering them with bits of gravel and sand and by the sheer force of the moving water.

- **Every river** carries sediment, which consists of large stones rolled along the riverbed, sand bounced along the bed and fine silt that floats in the water.

- **The discharge of a river** is the amount of water flowing past a particular point each second.

- **Rivers that flow** only after heavy rainstorms are "intermittent." Rivers that flow all year round are "perennial"—they are kept going between rains by water flowing from underground.

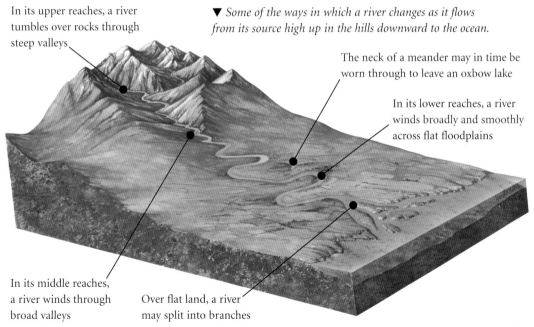

In its upper reaches, a river tumbles over rocks through steep valleys

▼ *Some of the ways in which a river changes as it flows from its source high up in the hills downward to the ocean.*

The neck of a meander may in time be worn through to leave an oxbow lake

In its lower reaches, a river winds broadly and smoothly across flat floodplains

In its middle reaches, a river winds through broad valleys

Over flat land, a river may split into branches

5

River channels

- **A channel** is the long trough along which a river flows.

- **When a river's channel** winds or has a rough bed, friction slows the river down.

- **A river flows faster** through a narrow, deep channel than a wide, shallow one because there is less friction.

- **All river channels** tend to wind, and the nearer they are to sea level, the more they wind. They form remarkably regular horseshoe-shaped bends called meanders.

- **Meanders** seem to develop because of the way in which a river erodes and deposits sediments.

▼ River channels come to an end when they reach the mouth where the water flows into a larger river, lake, or ocean.

▲ *The river here is so wide and flat, and its bed is so rough, that the water's flow is slowed by friction.*

- **One key factor** in meanders is the ups and downs along the river called pools (deeps) and riffles (shallows).

- **The distance between pools and riffles,** and the size of meanders, are in close proportion to the river's width.

- **Another key factor** in meanders is the tendency of river water to flow not only straight downstream but also across the channel. Water spirals through the channel in a corkscrew fashion called helicoidal flow.

- **Helicoidal flow** makes water flow faster on the outside of bends, wearing away the bank. It flows more slowly on the inside, building up deposits called slip-off slopes.

...FASCINATING FACT...
Meanders can form almost complete loops
with only a neck of land separating the ends.

River valleys

- **Rivers carve out valleys** as they wear away their channels.

- **High up in the mountains,** much of a river's energy goes into carving into the riverbed. The valleys there are deep, with steep sides.

- **Down** toward the ocean, more of a river's erosive energy goes into wearing away its banks. It carves out a broader valley as it winds back and forth.

- **Large meanders** normally develop only when a river is crossing broad plains in its lower reaches.

- **Incised meanders** are meanders carved into deep valleys. The meanders formed when the river was flowing across a low plain. The plain was lifted up and the river cut down into it, keeping its meanders.

- **The Grand Canyon** is made of incised meanders. They were created as the Colorado River cut into the Colorado Plateau after it was uplifted 17 million years ago.

- **The shape of a river valley** depends partly on the structure of the rocks over which it is flowing.

◀ Snake-like bends in a river's course are called meanders. They are often only separated by a narrow strip of land.

▲ *Rivers carve out valleys over hundreds of thousands of years as they grind material along their beds.*

- **Some valleys** seem far too big for their river alone to have carved them. Such a river is "underfit," or "misfit."

- **Many large valleys** with misfit rivers were carved out by glaciers or glacial meltwaters.

- **The world's rivers** wear the entire land surface down by an average of 3 in (8 cm) every 1,000 years.

Seas

- **Seas** are small oceans, completely enclosed or partly enclosed by land.

- **Seas** are shallower than oceans and do not have any major currents flowing through them.

- **In the Mediterranean** and other seas, tides can set up a seiche—a standing wave that sloshes back and forth like a ripple running up and down a bathtub.

- **If the natural** wave cycle of a seiche is different from the ocean tides, the tides are cancelled out.

- **If the natural** wave cycle of a seiche is similar to the ocean tides, the tides are magnified.

- **Scientists thought that** the Mediterranean was a dry desert 6 million years ago. They believed it was 9,842 ft (3,000 m) lower than it is today, and covered in salts.

▲ *The warm waters of the Mediterranean attract tourists to the coast of Spain.*

- **Recent evidence** from microfossils suggests that the Mediterranean was never completely dry.

- **Warm seas such as the Mediterranean** lose much more water by evaporation than they gain from rivers. So a current of water flows in steadily from the ocean.

- **Warm seas** lose so much water by evaporation that they are usually much saltier than the open ocean.

▼ *Waves in enclosed seas tend to be much smaller than those in the open ocean, because there is less space for them to develop.*

...FASCINATING FACT...
The Dead Sea is the lowest sea on Earth,
1,312 ft (400 m) below sea level.

Pacific Ocean

- **The Pacific** is the world's largest ocean. It is twice as large as the Atlantic and covers over one third of the world—70 million sq mi (181 million sq km) in area.

- **It is over 14,913 mi (24,000 km)** across from Panama to the Malay Peninsula—more than halfway round the world.

- **The word "pacific"** means calm. The ocean got its name from the 16th-century Portuguese explorer Magellan who was lucky enough to find gentle winds.

- **The Pacific is dotted** with thousands of islands. Some are the peaks of undersea volcanoes. Others are coral reefs sitting on top of the peaks.

▲ *There are thousands of low lying islands in the Pacific. Most are only about 3 ft (1 m) above sea level.*

◀ The coastal waters of California are rich in petroleum—the most important mineral resource of the Pacific.

- **The Pacific** has some of the greatest tides in the world (over 29.5 ft/9 m off Korea). Its smallest tide (just 1 ft/0.3 m) is on Midway Island in the Pacific.

- **On average,** the Pacific Ocean is 13,799 ft (4,200 m) deep.

- **Around the rim** there are deep ocean trenches including the world's deepest, the Mariana Trench.

- **A huge** undersea mountain range called the East Pacific Rise stretches from Antarctica up to Mexico.

- **The floor of the Pacific** is spreading along the East Pacific Rise at the rate of 4.7–6.3 in (12–16 cm) per year.

- **The Pacific** has more seamounts (undersea mountains) than any other ocean.

Atlantic Ocean

▲ *The damp, cool climate of the northern Atlantic frequently turns its waters steely gray.*

- **The Atlantic Ocean** is the second largest ocean, with an area of 31.6 million sq mi (82 million sq km). It covers one-fifth of the world's surface.

- **At its widest point,** between Spain and Mexico, the Atlantic is 5,965 mi (9,600 km) across.

- **The Atlantic** was named by the ancient Romans after the Atlas Mountains of North Africa.

- **There are very few islands** in the main part of the Atlantic Ocean. Most lie close to the continents.

- **On average,** the Atlantic is about 12,000 ft (3,660 m) deep.

- **The deepest point** in the Atlantic is the Puerto Rico Trench off Puerto Rico, which is 28,372 ft (8648 m) deep.

- **The Mid-Atlantic Ridge** is a great undersea ridge which splits the seabed in half. Along this ridge, the Atlantic is growing wider by 0.8–1.5 in (2–4 cm) every year.

- **Islands** in the mid-Atlantic are volcanoes that lie along the Mid-Atlantic Ridge, such as the Azores and Ascension Island.

- **The Sargasso Sea** is a huge area of water in the western Atlantic. It is famous for its floating seaweed.

- **The Atlantic** is a youngish ocean, about 150 million years old.

▲ *The Atlantic Ocean provides around a quarter of the world's catch of fish.*

15

Indian Ocean

▼ *Many of the Indian Ocean's islands have coral beaches.*

- **The Indian Ocean** is the third largest ocean. It is about half the size of the Pacific Ocean and covers one fifth of the world's ocean area. It has a total area of 28,349,937 sq mi (73,426,000 sq km).

- **The average depth** of the Indian Ocean is 12,762 ft (3,890 m).

- **The deepest point** is the Java Trench off Java, Indonesia, which is 24,442 ft (7,450 m) deep. It marks the line where the Australian plate is being subducted under the Eurasian plate.

16

- **The Indian Ocean** is 6,214 mi (10,000 km) across at its widest point, between Africa and Australia.

- **Scientists believe** that the Indian Ocean began to form about 200 million years ago when Australia broke away from Africa, followed by India.

- **The Indian Ocean** is getting 7.8 in (20 cm) wider every year.

- **The Indian Ocean** is scattered with thousands of tropical islands such as the Seychelles and Maldives.

- **The Maldives** are so low lying that they may be swamped if global warming melts the polar ice.

- **Unlike in other oceans,** currents in the Indian Ocean change course twice a year. They are blown by monsoon winds toward Africa in winter, and then in the other direction toward India in summer.

- **The Persian Gulf** is the warmest sea in the world; the Red Sea is the saltiest.

▶ *In the warm waters of the Indian Ocean coral reefs flourish.*

17

Arctic Ocean

▲ *Icebreakers are able to smash their way through sea ice using the strength of their reinforced bows.*

- **Most of the Arctic Ocean** is permanently covered with a vast floating raft of sea ice.

- **Temperatures** are low all year round, averaging –22°F (–30°C) in winter and sometimes dropping to –94°F (–70°C).

- **During the long winters,** which last more than four months, the Sun never rises above the horizon.

18

- **The Arctic** gets its name from arctos, the Greek word for "bear," because the Great Bear constellation is above the North Pole.

- **There are three kinds of sea ice** in the Arctic: polar ice, pack ice, and fast ice.

- **Polar ice** is the raft of ice that never melts through.

- **Polar ice** may be as thin as 6 ft (2 m) in places in summer, but in winter it is up to 165 ft (50 m) thick.

- **Pack ice** forms around the edge of the polar ice and only freezes completely in winter.

- **The ocean swell** breaks and crushes the pack ice into chunky ice blocks and fantastic ice sculptures.

- **Fast ice** forms in winter between pack ice and the land around the Arctic Ocean. It gets its name because it is held fast to the shore. It cannot move up and down with the ocean as the pack ice does.

▲ *The seal is one of the few creatures that can survive the bitter cold of the Arctic winter.*

Southern Ocean

- **The Southern Ocean** is the world's fourth largest ocean. It stretches all the way around Antarctica, and has an area of 13,500,000 sq mi (35,000,000 sq km).

- **It is the only ocean** that stretches all around the world.

- **In winter** over half the Southern Ocean is covered with ice and icebergs that break off the Antarctic ice sheet.

- **The East Wind Drift** is a current that flows counterclockwise around Antarctica close to the coast.

- **Further out** from the coast of Antarctica, the Antarctic circumpolar current flows in the opposite direction—clockwise from west to east.

- **The circumpolar current** carries more water than any other current in the world.

▲ *Many penguins such as the Emperor, the world's largest penguin, live on the ice floes of the Southern Ocean.*

▲ *Beneath the surface of the Antarctic ice, the sea temperature reaches just 28.4°F (–2°C). The freezing water is also a rich source of krill—tiny shrimp-like creatures.*

...FASCINATING FACT...
The circumpolar current could fill the Great Lakes in North America in just 48 hours.

- **The "Roaring Forties"** is the band between 40° and 50° South latitude. Within this band strong westerly winds blow unobstructed around the world.

- **The waves in the "Roaring Forties"** are the biggest in the world, sometimes higher than a ten-story building.

- **Sea ice** forms in round pieces called pancake ice.

Beaches

- **Beaches** are sloping bands of sand, shingle, or pebbles along the edge of a sea or lake.

- **Some beaches** are made entirely of broken coral or shells.

- **On a steep beach,** the backwash after each wave is strong. It washes material down the beach and so makes the beach gentler sloping.

- **On a gently sloping beach,** each wave runs in powerfully and falls back gently. Material gets washed up the beach, making it steeper.

...FASCINATING FACT...
The world's largest pleasure beach is Virginia Beach, Virginia, over 28 mi (45 km) long.

▶ *Waves crashing against the shore can weaken cliffs and cause some to fall into the ocean.*

▲ *The little bays in this beach have been scooped out as waves strike the beach at an angle.*

- **The slope of a beach** matches the waves, so the slope is often gentler in winter when the waves are stronger.

- **A storm beach** is a ridge of gravel and pebbles flung high above the normal high-tide mark during a storm.

- **At the top of each beach** a ridge, or berm, is often left at the high-tide mark.

- **Beach cusps** are tiny bays in the sand that are scooped out along the beach when waves strike it at an angle.

- **Many scientists** believe that beaches are only a temporary phenomenon caused by the changes in sea levels after the last Ice Age.

23

Coasts

- **Coastlines** are changing all the time as new waves roll in and out and tides rise and fall every six hours or so. Over longer periods coastlines are reshaped by the action of waves and the corrosion of salty water.

- **On exposed coasts** where waves strike the high rocks, they undercut the slope to create steep cliffs and headlands. Often waves can penetrate into the cliff to open up sea caves or blast through arches. When a sea arch collapses, it leaves behind tall pillars called stacks which may be worn away to stumps.

- **Waves work** on rocks in two ways. First, the rocks are pounded with a huge weight of water filled with stones. Second, the waves force air into cracks in the rocks with such force that the rocks split apart.

- **The erosive power** of waves is focused in a narrow band at wave height. So as waves wear away ocean cliffs, they leave the rock below wave height untouched. As cliffs retreat, the waves slice away a broad shelf of rock called a wave-cut platform. Water left behind in dips when the tide falls forms rockpools.

- **On more sheltered coasts,** the ocean may pile up sand into beaches (see beaches). The sand has been washed down by rivers or worn away from cliffs.

- **When waves hit** a beach at an angle, they fall straight back down the beach at a right angle. Any sand and shingle that the waves carry fall back slightly farther along the beach. In this way sand and shingle are moved along the beach in a zig-zag fashion. This is called longshore drift.

- **On beaches** prone to longshore drift, low fences called groins are often built to stop the sand from being washed away along the beach.

- **Longshore drift** can wash sand out across bays and estuaries to create sand bars called spits.

- **Bays** are broad indents in the coast with a headland on each side. Waves reach the headlands first, focusing their energy here. Material is worn away from the headlands and washed into the bay, forming a bay-head beach.

- **A cove is a small bay.** A bight is a huge bay, such as the Great Australian Bight. A gulf is a long narrow bight. The world's biggest bay is Hudson Bay, Canada, which has a shoreline 7,623 mi (12,268 km) long. The Bay of Bengal in India is larger in area.

▼ *The main features of a coastline.*

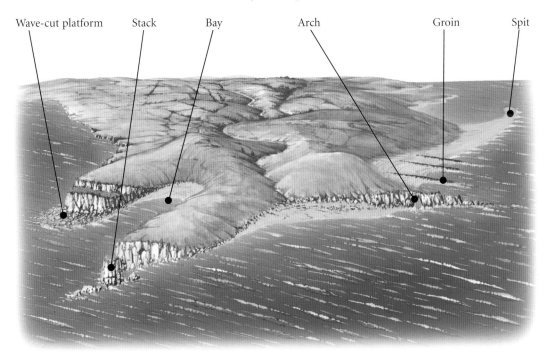

Wave-cut platform   Stack   Bay   Arch   Groin   Spit

Waves

- **Waves in the ocean** are formed when wind blows across the ocean and whips the surface into ripples.

- **Water particles** are dragged a short way by the friction between air and water, which is known as wind stress.

- **If the wind continues to blow** long and strong enough in the same direction, moving particles may build up into a ridge of water. At first this is a ripple, then a wave.

- **Waves seem to move** but the water in them stays in the same place, rolling around like rollers on a conveyor belt.

- **The size of a wave** depends on the strength of the wind and how far it blows over the water (the fetch).

▲ *When waves enter shallow water, the water in them piles up until eventually they spill over at the top and break.*

- **If the fetch is short,** the waves may simply be a chaotic, choppy "sea." If the fetch is long, they may develop into a series of rolling waves called a swell.

- **One in 300,000 waves** is four times bigger than the rest.

- **The biggest waves** occur south of South Africa.

- **When waves** move into shallow water, the rolling of the water is impeded by the seabed. The water piles up, then spills over in a breaker.

Tsunamis

- **Tsunamis** are huge waves that begin when the sea floor is violently shaken by an earthquake, a landslide, or a volcanic eruption.

- **In deep water** tsunamis travel almost unnoticeably below the surface. However, once they reach shallow coastal waters they rear up into waves 100 ft (30 m) high or higher.

- **Tsunamis** are often mistakenly called "tidal waves," but they are nothing to do with tides. The word tsunami (soon-army) is Japanese for "harbor wave."

- **Tsunamis** usually come in a series of a dozen or more—anything from five minutes to one hour apart.

▼ *Tsunamis do little damage in open water but can cause huge amounts of damage in shallow waters and inland.*

A shift in the seabed sends
out a pulse of water

As the pulse moves into shallow
water it rears into a giant wave

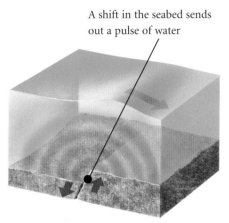
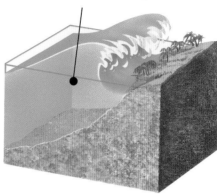

▲ *Tsunamis may be generated underwater by an earthquake, then travel far along the seabed before emerging to swamp a coast.*

- **Before a tsunami arrives,** the ocean may recede dramatically, like water draining from a bath.

- **Tsunamis can travel** along the seabed as fast as a jet plane, at 435 mph (700 km/h) or more.

- **Tsunamis** arrive within 15 minutes from a local quake.

- **A tsunami** generated by an earthquake in Japan might swamp San Francisco, 10 hours later.

- **The biggest tsunami** ever recorded was an 279-ft (85-m) high wave which struck Japan on April 24, 1771.

- **Tsunami warnings** are issued by the Pacific Tsunami Warning Center in Honolulu.

Tides

- **Tides are the way** the ocean rises a little then falls back every 12 hours or so.

- **When the tide is flowing** it is rising. When the tide is ebbing it is falling.

- **Tides are caused** by the pull of gravity between the Earth, Moon, and Sun.

- **The mutual pull** of the Moon's and the Earth's gravity stretches the Earth into an egg shape.

- **The solid Earth** is so rigid that it stretches only 8 in (20 cm).

- **Ocean waters** can flow freely over the Earth to create two tidal bulges (high tides) of water. One bulge is directly under the Moon, the other is on the far side of the Earth.

High tides happen at the same time each day on opposite sides of the Earth

▼ At high tide, the ocean rises up the shore and dumps seaweed, shells, and drift wood. Most coasts have two high tides and two low tides every day.

At high tide the water level rises

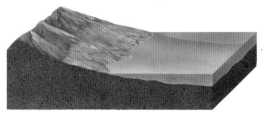

At low tide the water level goes down again

● **As the Earth rotates** every 24 hours the tidal bulges stay in the same place under the Moon. Each place on the ocean has high tide twice a day. The Moon is moving as well as the Earth, making high tides occur not once every 12 hours but once every 12 hours 25 minutes.

● **The continents** get in the way, making the tidal bulges slosh around in a complex way. As a result the timing and height of tides vary enormously. In the open ocean tides rise only 3 ft (1 m) or so, but in enclosed spaces such as the Bay of Fundy, in Nova Scotia, Canada they rise over 50 ft (15 m).

● **The Sun is much farther away** than the Moon, but it is so big that its gravity has an effect on the tides.

● **The Moon and the Sun** line up at a Full and a New Moon, creating high spring tides twice a month. When the Moon and Sun pull at right angles at a Half Moon, they cause neap tides which are lower than normal tides.

▶ *Neap tides occur when the Sun and Moon are at right angles to each other and pulling in different directions.*

▶ *Spring tides occur when the Sun and the Moon are lined up and pulling together.*

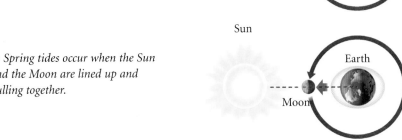

31

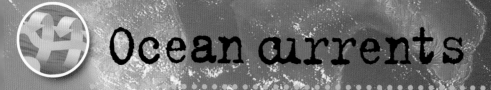

Ocean currents

▲ *Ocean currents start as wind blows across the water's surface.*

- **Ocean surface currents** are like giant rivers, often tens of miles wide, 328 ft (100 m) deep, and flowing at 9 mph (15 km/h).

- **The major currents** are split on either side of the Equator into giant rings called gyres.

- **In the Northern Hemisphere** the gyres flow round clockwise; in the south they flow counterclockwise.

- **Ocean currents** are driven by a combination of winds and the Earth's rotation.

- **Near the Equator** water is driven by easterly winds (see wind) to make westward-flowing equatorial currents.

- **When equatorial currents** reach continents, the Earth's rotation deflects them poleward as warm currents.

- **As warm currents flow** poleward, westerly winds drive them east back across the oceans. When the currents reach the far side, they begin to flow toward the Equator along the west coasts of continents as cool currents.

- **The North Atlantic Drift** brings so much warm water from the Caribbean to SW England that it is warm enough to grow palm trees, yet it is as far north as Newfoundland.

- **By drying out the air** cool currents can create deserts, such as California's Baja and Chile's Atacama deserts.

Wave movement

Surface currents

Underwater currents

▶ *The wind sets the surface waters in motion as currents. Waves create swirling circular currents, while deeper currents run beneath the surface.*

. . . .**FASCINATING FACT**. . . .
The West Wind Drift around Antarctica moves
2,000 times as much water as the Amazon.

33

Deep ocean currents

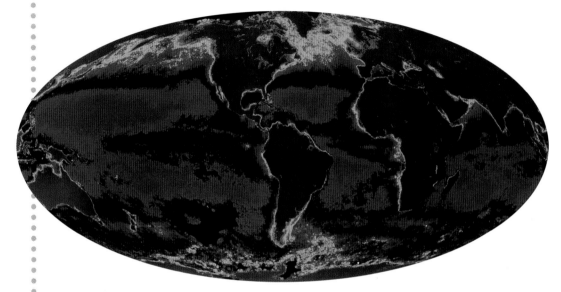

▲ *This satellite picture shows variations in ocean surface temperature.*

- **Ocean surface currents** (see ocean currents) affect only the top 328 ft (100 m) or so of the ocean. Deep currents involve the whole ocean.

- **Deep currents** are set in motion by differences in the density of seawater. They move only a few metres a day.

- **Most deep currents** are called thermohaline circulations because they depend on the water's temperature ("thermo") and salt content ("haline").

- **If seawater** is cold and salty, it is dense and sinks.

- **Typically, dense water** forms in the polar regions. Here the water is cold and weighed down by salt left behind when ocean ice forms.

- **Dense polar water** sinks and spreads out toward the Equator deep below the surface.

- **Oceanographers** call dense water that sinks and starts deep ocean currents "deep water."

- **In the Northern Hemisphere** the main area for the formation of deep water is the North Atlantic.

- **Dense salty water** from the Mediterranean pours deep down very fast: 3 ft (1 m) p/sec, through the Straits of Gibraltar to add to the North Atlantic deep water.

- **There are three levels** in the ocean: the "epilimnion" (the surface waters warmed by sunlight, up to 328–984 ft/100–300 m down); the "thermocline," where it becomes colder quickly with depth; and the "hypolimnion," the bulk of deep, cold ocean water.

▲ *In the polar regions the waters become colder and saltier which makes them heavier. They sink and spread slowly toward the Equator.*

Ocean deeps

- **The oceans** are over 6,561 ft (2,000 m) deep on average.

- **Along the edge** of the ocean is a ledge of land—the continental shelf. The average sea depth here is 426 ft (130 m).

- **At the edge of the continental shelf** the seabed plunges thousands of feet steeply down the continental slope.

- **Underwater avalanches** roar down the continental slope at over 37 mph (60 km/h). They carve out deep gashes called submarine canyons.

- **The gently** sloping foot of the continental slope is called the continental rise.

- **Beyond the continental rise** the ocean floor stretches out in a plain called the abyssal plain. It lies as deep as 16,404 ft (5,000 m) below the water's surface.

▼ *Under the ocean there are mountains, plateaux, plains, and trenches similar to those found on land.*

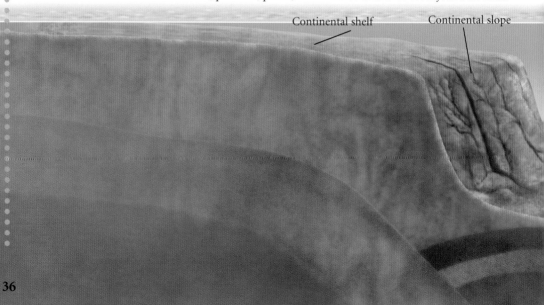

Continental shelf

Continental slope

● **The abyssal plain** is covered in a thick slime called ooze. It is made partly from volcanic ash and meteor dust and partly from the remains of sea creatures.

● **The abyssal plain** is dotted with huge mountains, thousands of feet high, called seamounts.

● **Flat-topped seamounts** are called guyots. They may be volcanoes that once projected above the surface.

● **The deepest places** in the ocean floor are ocean trenches—made when tectonic plates are driven down into the mantle. The Mariana Trench is 35,640 ft (10,863 m) deep.

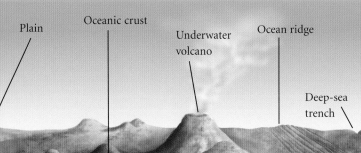

Plain

Oceanic crust

Underwater volcano

Ocean ridge

Deep-sea trench

▲ *Huge numbers of sea creatures live in the pelagic zone—the surface waters of the open ocean beyond the continental shelf.*

37

Black smokers

▲ *Black smokers were first discovered less than 30 years ago.*

● **Black smokers** are natural chimneys on the seabed. They billow black fumes of hot gases and water.

● **Black smokers** are technically known as hydrothermal vents. They are volcanic features.

● **Black smokers** form along mid-ocean ridges where the tectonic plates are moving apart.

● **Black smokers** begin when seawater seeps through cracks in the sea floor. The water is heated by volcanic magma, and it dissolves minerals from the rock.

● **Once the water is superheated,** it spews from the vents in scalding, mineral-rich black plumes.

● **The plume cools** rapidly in the cold sea, leaving behind thick deposits of sulphur, iron, zinc, and copper in tall, chimney-like vents.

● **The tallest vents** are 165 ft (50 m) high.

● **Water jetting** from black smokers can reach 1,223°F (662°C).

● **Smokers** are home to a community of organisms that thrive in the scalding waters and toxic chemicals. The organisms include giant clams and tube worms.

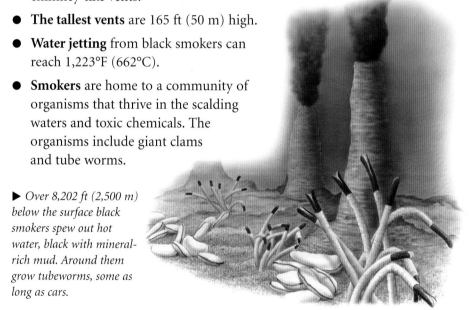

▶ *Over 8,202 ft (2,500 m) below the surface black smokers spew out hot water, black with mineral-rich mud. Around them grow tubeworms, some as long as cars.*

...FASCINATING FACT...
Each drop of sea water in the world circulates through a smoker every ten million years.

Index